# Bazar Oriental

# Bazar Oriental

Shqiponjë Ahmedi

RESOURCE *Publications* • Eugene, Oregon

BAZAR ORIENTAL

Copyright © 2022 Shqiponjë Ahmedi. All rights reserved. Except for brief quotations in critical publications or reviews, no part of this book may be reproduced in any manner without prior written permission from the publisher. Write: Permissions, Wipf and Stock Publishers, 199 W. 8th Ave., Suite 3, Eugene, OR 97401.

Resource Publications
An Imprint of Wipf and Stock Publishers
199 W. 8th Ave., Suite 3
Eugene, OR 97401

www.wipfandstock.com

PAPERBACK ISBN: 978-1-6667-4399-9
HARDCOVER ISBN: 978-1-6667-4400-2
EBOOK ISBN: 978-1-6667-4401-9

08/02/22

To my parents, who won't be able to understand a word.
Sorry I didn't write it in Albanian.

To my brothers Besi and Drini, for
making my life beautiful.

To the people who inspired me,
if you are wondering, the answer is yes.

Wine comes in at the mouth
And love comes in at the eye;
That's all we shall know for truth
Before we grow old and die.
I lift the glass to my mouth,
I look at you, and I sigh.

—William Butler Yeats

# Contents

Of Gibsons and Other Hurricanes | 1
Of Bazars | 55
Of Home | 101

# Introduction

Dear A.,

After the war everything was different. What was left of my uncle's house were blackened walls pierced by bullets and butterflies. The cold basement was a bedroom and a kitchen, there were no more pickled jars stored in there. Only people and their limping hearts. My friends were different too, they were quieter, their eyes matched their worn-out clothes and bare feet. We didn't play in the fields anymore, we played in the ruins. Hide and seek was no longer a game. The asphalted road we used to take to the ice cream shop had turned into a dirt road with leftover pieces of concrete and mourning. "The tanks ate it mercilessly" my uncle said. I did not know what "mercilessly" meant, but I heard that word a lot that summer. The grownups would talk softer when we were around, they said only one little girl survived, they said the soldiers let her live on purpose so she can tell of all the horrors. Fifty-eight to be exact. They said she hid on the bread granary. I kept imagining her tiny body crumpled like aluminum foil. It was a good summer, with the exception of the allergies I developed from the burned-down houses that served as our playground. It was the summer of freedom, although bleak, it was difficult to grasp it. First you had to peel off the anguish like old-fashioned floral wallpaper, you had to scrub it away like a sticky bar floor and dust off the rags still glued to our skins, but it was there, in our veins. It was there like sheep's flowers blooming in my childhood village. I do not recall the origins of the name; it was what we called the first flower before spring. I would carry warm bread and cheese that mother used to make and went hunting for this flower, the first sign that warmer days were lying ahead. This saffron yellow flower would bloom, proud and sweet, before the snow melted. Just as we love again, before the hurt is gone.

    Dear, forgive this digression, it is the thirteenth day of wildfires. My words like dew disperse before reaching you. The island itself is covered in flames, there isn't much any of us can do. Buckets of water are pathetic. In vain I call you to my succor. In vain I wait for you to arrive. People have started to recognize fear; they are holding their belongings close to their chests and pray. There's a lot of praying. Their tedious tumult, their devotions, overwhelm me. I have nothing dear to hold to my chest. Except for the lavender-scented ink and the dip pen with two falcon nibs that you gave me on Three Kings Day. I am trying not to waste too much paper because it is running out everywhere. That is why, aesthetics aside I am writing on both sides. My impious fingers are lilac now and they smell of lavender. It feels so long ago that they were pale and touching yours, laughing at the story of the mouse that drowned from its tears inside a perfume bottle. I wonder what has become of you. I wonder what has become of you. Perhaps, your misfortunes are crueler than mine. Oh, how greedy of me! To burden you with my fears and despair. Just the other day I thought of the times we would sip our yellow coffee sitting on the pavement, in that sunlit corner, gazing at local artists as they painted the church. And how dismayed we were, if our spot was occupied by others, as if we were paying rent for those afternoon sun rays. As if we had kidnapped the sun, warmer than our fingertips, warmer than virtues which strengthen tenderness. I laughed so vigorously at the memory that my own laughter saddened me. I do not know why. It saddened me to my core. It saddened me more than the thought of running out of paper and ink. It saddened me more than the day you disappointed me. This sadness is the only thing that keeps you close to me still. Oh, how I long for the silence which reigned our afternoons, reading in La Taverneta and swimming in January in a perfumed frozen sea.

Never yours,
S.

# Of Gibsons and Other Hurricanes.

I have found a broken human. We cover each other's lacerations with our bodies and Minion plasters. We love together sometimes. I have found a broken human. The epigraph of my voyage. His hair is the ocean. His rustic hands, his rustic hands.

## You (Part II)

You, my Anthropocene epoch,
my Great Acceleration, my *ottava rima*
You, who reconstructed me
from the brittle shards of my being
You, who sang "Duerme negrito"
when I could not sleep.
You, worthy of Aivazovsky's brush
or any brush for that matter.

You, my Dionysian mystery
reading the news on my velvety sweater
that surprisingly fits you
and me a Titan
"Turn down the music a little bit"
you say graciously
and I do
although the garbage trucks outside
are making more noise
than Ed Maverick and his fans.

You, my Dionysian mystery
Somehow, I can never crack my chest open
without the fear of Achlys
drowning me in darkness for centuries.

My Parnassian eyes drink this faultless night
Play the phorminx
as I walk out of their sick traditions.

## Arrivals

You arrived the way summer arrives
Unannounced
Suddenly I wake up kicking blankets
and sorrows on the floor
And the pillow between the thighs
that supports my curled-up state
And the heat
Lingers onto the flesh
Like a bad cough
It feeds on it like a mandurugo

You arrived the way
powdery summer nights arrive
In oversized white cotton t-shirts
Espadinha's "A revolta" playing on repeat
Bras shoved away with winter's garments
With a bundle of misery and
sweetness and violence-scented ink.

## This silly firmament

My loyal footsteps
Sail like clouds
Spilling tales of things lost
You stand in front of me
And I want to tell you things
Sweet things
About your soft warm mouth
And the little stubborn curls
Floating with the light
Now let us run
Now let us run
For Autumn is here
And chestnut woes are here
And wondrous thirst is here
And blue dusky days are here
And the pale clock
Is a giant
That enthrones
all the gold and all the burden.

## Ma'at

Could you wear the feather of truth?
Would it weigh on you for being unworthy?
Would it bend your back and eventually splinter it?
If I clutch your heart, would it be light enough
For you to make it to the field of reeds
Or would you be doomed in the nocturnal vault?

# Blue flax

The moon giggles
Taking off her gown
Clouds hang their laundry out to dry in the rubescent mere
Having popcorn covered in chimichurri with you
Having ramen in drenched gym clothes with you
You say I am your *chaska ñawi*
I look at you
And my heart blinks like a broken neon sign
of a Chinese-owned bar in Exiample.

### Zamba of things remembered

You have enslaved me
Just like the arrogant olive orchards
Have enslaved Andalusians of Jaén
Diaphanous enthrallment
Muffled kisses will blossom on your morning coffee
Fragrant cushions will rise at midnight
Outside the window
The cobalt hue of sobbing is gone
Let us bathe in elderflower cordial
Don't let me down.

## They water the plants of El Palace

Swirling lines of a Van Gogh painting
Graceful cypresses
Surround me
Like your absence
Your absence
Your absence
upsurges in my chest
like gulping dust in Playa de Bahía
Where you laughed so hard
At my almost death
that you got an asthmatic attack.

## Baudlaire's torment

I am drowning
in the limited-edition snorkeling mask
you got for me
I breathe underwater again
And again
Until all I can see is the sun rising
over Valencian fields
The heaviness, the heaviness.
Oh, are you worthy?
Are you worthy of my brush?

# Song of Lost Fridays

Yes, a woman
Rehearsing with arteries
in her nescient hands
Like drunken eyes
in Passeig del Born
Rimbaud's silence
has left a heritage in me
The moon tonight resembles
the luxury crêpe
Without ham
Irregular pieces of ice
In my refulgent space shoes
Swinging lights

There is everything
There is everyone
And there is you.

### Lilac T-shirt

I keep defying
I give myself a pep talk too
And the Earth under my feet
Rises and shoves me vehemently
And the sky and its creatures
encircle me

I play the fool
I greet them but they don't greet back
They summon the ocean bellowing
Jellyfish and Bartlett's anthias
glisten on its surface

I remain unyielding
My feet glued to the pomegranate floor
They summon the cobblestone
of my fatherland
And jostle me towards you
wrathfully.

## Of Gibsons and Other Hurricanes

My wretchedness
My ocean-haired lover
The three of us howl that song
Of the lunatic who
bit onto the edge of his glass
His bleeding lips blended with the wine
Wanting to exsanguinate drop by drop
The trail of venom that she left behind
My ocean-haired lover
You bought for me my first leather jacket
I was running home
In the pouring rain
Thinking what became of Barbara
and how much
it rained in Brest that day
Jumping on each puddle
The paper bag soaked and tattered
The jacket slid down in front of my feet
I wore it anyway
I was wearing rain and your fragrance
My ocean-haired lover
For you, I will ignore some of the monsters.

## Pierced Morals

In need of recollecting my truths
I am here
I am here
With a gauze compress on my right arm
The nurse said I should press on it
Press on it
for five years
or five minutes
Results in eight days
There is a man sleeping
on the left side of my bed
He has a million blue braids
His soul is inked more than his skin
He seems imperious
He likes to be held in silence
I do too
My shoes and the pockets
of my denim shorts
are full of sand
There is a shore on my floor
We had champagne cocktails
And whiskey after
An avocado stain on my bedsheets
The man on the left side of my bed moves
And a tropical cyclone emerges

He sleepily rests his arm on my stomach
The ink starts pouring into me like
the night pours its charm over *Ano Poli*
It drenches me
unhurriedly.

## Mad

I still touch my left breast
Every time a ginger head passes by
Especially if it's a baby
Even if it's hair dye
Just in case
I miss you.

## Blithering hours

Everything is not real
Fraudulent sighs
Fugitive hours
Chivalrous kisses on my hand
Blowing fleers
Bourbon, ginger and vanilla mischiefs
Malicious fingerprints
Everything is not real
Not as real as a rustle
Inside the walls of Alcazar.

## I once knew

I once knew a boy
Who could neither laugh too hard
Nor feel too sad
He had a quena planted in his chest
He always woke up soaked in joy
Touching his skin felt like old shoes
kicking little rocks
In an unpaved road
of a misplaced village
The shoes belong to a child
with dried chocolate
around the corners of the mouth
The child whistles
Just as your chest is whistling by my side.
I once knew a boy who held me
the way one holds a torn grocery bag pressed
against one's body to retain its contents
I once knew a boy who tied
my uncomfortable Docs
in Boadas
I once knew a boy who
was a former ant assassin.

## Our Little Future

Is full to the brim
Like Calvino's moon leaking
Silvery lust
On our bodies
And we crave more
We bite and scrape each other's thirst
We float in our renovated ocean
of raw longing
We dream of arms, of scents,
of Angostura kisses.
Our little future is just not so little
It is full of you
It is full of me
And we are theatrically abiding.

## Ancient warmth

You are the feeling of
Getting a new beret hat
In a stonewashed store in La Latina
On a drizzly day
Of adding a scarce magenta hue
Or a lettuce shade
To my infinite beret collection
I float on the river of your skin
I float on all the gin we have shared
I float on the curves of your voice
As you read Pizarnik to me
And our chests smell of coffee beans.

## Wish

I want to tell you
Sweet things
I want to tell you
But I don't know what
You see, the trees tickle this mad light
And I stand heavy
I want to tell you sweet things
But I don't know what.

## Untitled

Selkirk's solitude
Doesn't come close to mine
I thought
For mine is the solitude
Of a Proustian child
As if I were the ice
And you the glass
You shatter against me
Or I against you
Station down
Station down
I once wished to evaporate
In your acid
And turn into angel's share
But not anymore.

# Payada

Gaucho
Singing at the *pulperia*

*Mi caballo y mi mujer viajaron para Salta*

It's sunny but it's raining
A witch must have gotten married
you say
*Salud* to moving forward
*Salud* to looking back
Only long enough
To understand
And recover
And leave better

*El caballo que se vuelva*
*mi mujer que no me hace falta.*

## Mapuche Lover

Will I always wander
on the shores of Acheron
An iconoclast at times
Although I
I'll wear the bassaris
I declare
I'll strike you with my thyrsus
I'll be your maenad and tear you apart
In the holy plain of Thebes.

## The liqueur of absence

Are we really introverted planets,
Spitting chemicals at each other?
Fibers of sadness
Sunsets that resemble leftovers
of an apricot birthday cake
This proud city bowed its head
like the horse in Ludwig's
*Abschied der Auswanderer*

I am exhausted of showers
I want a bathtub
Let me dance with the naiads
Never stop stealing food for me
Please drown in my tragedy.

## Perfect day (Part II)

Listening to you
Ramble on about your day
Lying down in bed at last
All my fluttering pieces
Trapped like sheep's wool on barbed wire
In subway stations, screens, pillowcases
libraries and bars
Are finally finding their way back to me
And once in a while
I even begin to feel like myself again.

# Gifts

In May we were poor
We spent our last *pesos* to dazzle each other
For our birthdays which were one day apart
In May we were as poor as a church mouse
Had never felt wealthier.

## Green mornings

*That is not the way to kill a criollo*
Echoes from the kitchen
And your voice follows
Me, still in bed
Surrounded by pillows
and two black cats
Waiting for you
And the mate
you prepare every morning
You sit by the bed with a black
Calabash gourd
And begin the process of serving
This infused tea which is more than herbs
Something your father did for your mother
You were angry at your father
But "he did one thing right" you utter

It is less bitter each day
The tea that taught me, drinking from
the same *bombilla* with strangers
is not such a big deal
What matters is sharing
And we share
Greenish kisses
And we smell of earth
Of Guaraní pain
We smell of Río de la Plata

Of socialist theocracy,
of Jesuit reductions

And I will remember the way your mouth
domesticates my arms.

## Chats over coffee and cereal croissants

Remember the day
I told you about Aymara people
And how they believed
the future was behind them
For they could not see it
And the past in front of them
Because they could
You thought it absurd
And I was convinced
They were right
And in my madness
I convinced you too.

## Fear

A wreath of laurel
From the Vale of Tempe
Is all I ask for
If that is too much to ask for
Your hand shall suffice
Let us march out of here
I can teach you how
To be unafraid of sorrow.

# Gauchoesque

Join me
In my freedom
In my misery
The world is on the verge
Of a miscarriage
Let us celebrate
This ignominious downfall
Tonight, I am in the mood
To salute our destruction
I can hear laughter
And crystal glasses clinking
There, I see Klimt and Schiele
Maar and Limba
At Café de la Place Blanche
Camus and Breton
At Les Deux Magots
Éluard, Gala and Max
"This has been surreal"
"A toast" cries Dalí,
Bursting into the room
in his bathrobe
and espadrilles
"A toast to staying home"
"To social distancing, folks"
And silence
I freeze them in an image
I cannot breathe

I reach for the window
Silence barges in
Pressing unkindly on my chest
And none of them
can help me now.

## Your hands

Your hands have held souls
I can feel it in the coarse texture
No weightlifting can leave your skin
as hardened as souls can

Your hands have clenched hearts
and caressed hair that scarred them
Your hands have touched and sinned
Your hands have mixed spices and spirits

Your hands have turned pages
and stroked words
Your hands have crushed
and broken things
Your hands have bruised
and cured cities

Your hands have wiped tears
on unfamiliar faces
Your hands have mended cracks
on different veins

Your hands have insulted
Your hands have held the planets together
until they reconciled again
Your hands have made promises
to hold other hands ceaselessly

Your hands have shattered all the vows
Your hands have stolen for me

And here they are
Squeezing my body
They are still earnest and accurate
and full of art

And here they are
Keeping me sane and warm.

## Perfect day (Part I)

Getting drunk
Going on a Joyce Crawl
In Piazza Ponterosso 3
Via San Nicolo 31
Via Giovanni Boccaccio 1
Stopping
Staring at you
Uttering
'What an adventure
meeting you has been'
Gruffly pulling me towards you
Sinking your sleepy
fingers in my hair
Kissing me with the yearning
of the Bayamo wind
Shouting *Caruso*
at the top of our lungs.

My broken human is just too broken. His scathe ran me over like gritty skateboard wheels against the floral tiles of this city. I confused you with a beginning. My broken human, I must say goodbye, or I won't make it home.

## Leaves

These blue walls
Cycle with flat tires on my wounds
I touched you
With an alchemist's hunger
To turn you into something
Anything
Funny it seems
You even participated
Now, why did you?
These old blue walls
Of this sanctuary
Bring no peace
To my disturbed cells.

## Plush toys

Being in bed with someone
And feeling stiflingly lonely
Is the skill
Our generation
Will be remembered for.

## Not very dark and stormy

Not very dark
And not very stormy
I know that now
I know
that watching the tempest
with only your eyelids as a shield
is bravery
or imprudence
I didn't mind being imprudent
Not when it comes
To you.

## Fasting

I don't eat lately
My stomach
is full of despair
Full of autumn leaves
and rakes with no tines
My stomach
is a wrinkled fitted bedsheet
Where socks get stuck
Where gloom
has taken refuge
My stomach
has your first bicycle in it
My stomach
is full of your childhood ghosts
I don't eat lately
I miss you.

## To Marquéz

And he said *more*
Like Dario in his autumnal song
More olives
More music
More silver skin onions
Eighteenth century chivalry
Throws and pours
And overfills and refills
Garnishes with his infantile spirit
More poetry
More potato chips
More mini chocolates
He allows me to be his Hathor
His Eye of Ra
His pagan in exile
*Eres linda y hechicera*
He quotes awe-inspiring words
And he almost let me down.

## Silky little mornings

It makes me sad
To think that
We shall run out of time
Before you get to meet me
In Calle de Barco
In Café de la Luz.

## You (Part III)

Yes, it terrifies me
As if the minute it falls out of my lips
It will rebound off a surface
Like a ricochet bullet
Killing me instantly.

So, I stare at my cup of tea
Hoping you did not notice my blushing
I tell you
There are two kinds of people
The ones that smell of home
And the ones that reek
of the Tsukiji fish market

Hoping you will listen between the lines
And see that you are home to me
That nothing chortles louder
than your fingers on my skin.

## Invitation

Come and stab me with your pearl hair sticks
Play "La Tristecita" for me
I miss you.

## Little lifetime

I am here pretending
To imagine what it feels like
What it is going to feel like
When you are no longer here
I know I won't wake up
To muezzin's morning call
Announcing your death
Because you won't be dead
Merely gone.

### Last word

Metal against metal
Ice against glass
Stainless steel against
microfiber cleaning cloths
Bitters slide between the smithereens
You put a maraschino cherry
on top of my reason
And your arm around my drink.

## Take this pain

Take this pain to spice up your breakfast
Spread it on your salmon bagel
Mix it in your matcha tea
Throw it on top of your organic oats
along with the chia seeds
Take this pain
For a run along the seashore
To the dreadful stair master
Take this pain and wrap it up
in the blanket that you bought
when you thought you were finally home
Let it suffocate in it
Drag this pain with you
Exhaust it
Until it decides to leave
Until it has no more darkness
to feed from
Until his name remains
just an error in your
acknowledgements page
Take this pain
As if it were supplements
For there will be other failures
But not ones that can defeat your soul
Not like this
Never like this.

## You (Part IV)

My Dionysian misery
Every trivial sigh that I make
Becomes a dithyramb
In front of you.

## Mission: separation

Let us start another round
I will have to be an engineer,
an architect
to tell them exactly how to position
their hand on my forehead,
how to position their body holding mine,
the level of closeness
In meticulous detail
I will have to teach them
how to behave when we see ginger heads
I will carry your legacy with me
and splash the next person with it generously,
so that they may resemble you
How could I ever?
Something is not right
*Patchouli ardent* doesn't sit right on their skin
Their hand
is too heavy on my stomach
The heat
coming out of their body
makes me want to dive
into a pool of oleander
Is that what you call a softener?
What about the little violet grains for extra smell?
Never thought of it?
Why don't they ever want
to see Independence Day

or point at sausage dogs passing by?
This, this cannot be right
How long will it take for me to ruin them
and restitch them into the things we were
And then leave them because
they remind me of you a little too much
Is this longing or madness?

## Lightweight

Do not place anything in my luggage
Nothing that could connect you and I
Nothing that could remind me
of another misfortune
None of our ghosts
Sure, it hurts
Whatever is left inside my chest
Withers like a roasted sweet potato
Forgotten in a food truck
at the end of the day
It is quite cold here
Sure, it hurts
And it had to be you
the one to remind me of dying
There are styles of pains
that no *chacarera* can heal
It hurts, sure it does
Now let me go
Hand luggage only
Because this damn plague
weighs *un monton*.

# Of Bazars.

# Souls

*Inspired by Besian Ahmeti's "Paris".*

It was you, just you, not the poetry, not even me
Everything came back to me in pieces
The waiting,
The grey stations embroidered with yearning
Your hand in mine
"Can I sit next to you to see the thunder?"
"Certainly"
Our knees touch and I feel you
It is too soon to feel you
It is too soon to feel you
Bread and cheese, up the hills
Running with the shadows
The warm bread in our cold cold fingers
"Let us steal some cherries"
"They are still yellow and green"
"I will be the guard"
"Run, run, run"
Now he is dying,
He has got a few months to live they say
The one who chased us, the one we called names
The one who waited for the cherries to turn red
Contempt in her eyes
I desperately want her approval
Maybe if she sees the way you gaze at me,
maybe just maybe

"We are the rotten crowd" I think to myself,
and your heart is too warm.
"Let us be friends . . . I want to dance now"
The waves, the wind
The beach towels wrapped around my shoulders
You
And
Me wrapped around your shoulders
An embrace,
Uncontrollable sobbing
"This means no, does it not?"
It was you, just you,
Not the cherries,
Not the wild, scorching summers
Not the bruised souls
Not even me.

## Sweetheart, you must be the jester

Words and silence and more silence
The chair keeps spinning
A solitary house and a lake
A boat too
A wall painted red
Wasn't that the reason you rented the place?
Words within you
Silence within me
You and the dictionary
Flipping pages, letters, planets
You want to say so much
"Sunny" on Kosmos
It's so early, so bright
A broken wine glass
Replaced by another the next day
Not quite the same
But we drink
Until the night is so amused
"I can feel you"
I hit my head against a crystalline window
Trying to replace our broken wine glass
And came to you holding a soda can on my forehead
You put honey instead
This waltz, this time
I'm wearing your army jumper
We are in the kitchen,
I wrap my arms around you

"I will stay one more day"
Chet Baker with "A taste of honey" on Kosmos
And all that jazz
I'm wearing the t-shirt your ex bought you
Laughing madly as you carry me on your back
We stop at the spinning chair
Your fingers move the curls from my face and
you stare deep inside my ridiculous heart
"Always run to me darling."

You are not decent for my soul. Now I have to learn gardening. I have to skillfully uproot the words you carelessly threw into my bloodstream and all the dancing sewn into my limbs. I have to pick the right tools too. And spare enough flesh and blood to make it home.

## Wintry rosemary

We are the winds
That carry heavy rains
What do you mean really?
We met
Because you were bored in Athens
And I was in pain
And I can almost hear you say
'Sometimes you are so ridiculous darling'
Inhale
Allow me to touch your essence
Allow me to heal some and bruise some
Exhale
I meant
We are the souls
That carry hefty storms
and unspectacular misery
While the monotonic solace remains
'We are earthborn after all'.

### I'm going to love you

Love you so awkwardly
It might leave you with bruises
you never notice
until someone points them out
Love you so severely
You shall be convinced
It's the first time I've ever loved
And probably the last
You're going to be convinced that
you are the person who taught me how to love
(oh, such an incorruptible thing to teach)
I am going to love you
in all my favorite ways
In all the ways I've been loved
In all the ways I haven't been loved
I'm going to change two sometimes
three or four trains to get to you
Just to taste your mouth for one minute
And take the same trains back
Before the saliva from your lips
blends with my breath
My skin will remember your every sigh
My hair will remember
the very texture of your fingers
in quiet midnights
and tangled limbs
I'm going to love you so tenderly

It's going to feel like waking up
from a peaceful sleep at the beach,
feeling the mild, clean,
soap-like smell of dusk
It's going to feel like
that pure honorable moment
of being grateful to be alive
when snowflakes waltz around you
and land on your eyelashes
I'm going to love you unfathomably
Like old childhood reveries
hidden underneath your mattress
I'm going to witness every scar on your body
and immerse myself
in every story related to each disfigurement,
I will shape every hurtful memory
with my bare hands
until any pain that may still linger like an apparition
becomes mine instead
I'm going to love you drunkenly
The way I love beer and wine
drunk straight out of the bottle
by the sea or in round little tables
in cobblestone streets
listening to lyrics half translated
that I'll never understand
but pretend that I do just a little
because you are trying so hard
I'm going to smash my own heart
like a piggy bank and release all the light
it has collected for twenty-seven years
so that you can bathe in it

I'm going to love you the way I loved
Huckleberry Finn and Jim when I was twelve
I'm going to love you
Until you see yourself

And then I'll disappear like a zephyr
You will feel me in the white sheer curtain
of your bedroom dancing the way I danced in your arms
The night we met
And you'll wonder if anything was ever real
If I was ever real
I was
We were.

## Agonizingly fleeting

Our hearts shall begin to shriek
And we shall press our fists heavily
And shush them
We shall have coconut ice-cream
And say goodbye
As if we never
Sketched maps
On each other's skin.

### Lu & Leslie were here

It should not be so damn baffling
I asked if you were happy
Not if quantum entanglement intrigues you
Not if superluminal speeds
Remind you of poverty in Liberia

And Lu
She does not know
That Leslie wrote her name on a toilet door
Somewhere in a pedestrian bar
Because she is so wistfully unworldly
It rained so much that night
I could not really tell
if we were happy.

## Thirst-land

You look at me and mock me
for always stirring the coffee
even though I never put any sugar in
I think about how much
I miss my mother's fig jam
The jars
In the cold storage room
That scares me still

It is sweet
Like tenderness and the idyllic feeling
of watching tiny raindrops
on a café window when you have
just arrived in a new country
and butter croissants
like petite crescent moons
warmly tickle your nose
Just before grief begins to decant itself
In your creases.

## Red wool

She cried like there is no shame
in crying
And my heart did not break
It just cracked a little
Probably like Rembrandt's heart
when he watched Saskia suffering.

## Not like Sunday morning

We slow danced to
"Broken Bicycles" the night I departed.

We were fools nothing more
Two riant fools who dreamed
Way too much
We got scorched to the ground
Like timeworn,
unrecyclable Christmas decorations.

## A mouthful of wine

My poetry is too small
Too petty
To contain you
And all the ways you worshipped me
My poetry is too small
Too uninviting
To depict everything you are
Correction *were**
My poetry is too small
Too non-existent
To keep you alive
My poetry is not poetry
When you are in it
And sadly, you are in all of it.

# Theatrical horrors of the stars (Part I)

Last night was unusual
I thought I was made up of constellations
I almost sent you that pitiable poem
I have missed you before, in a sane way
(If there is a sane way to miss someone that is)
Last night I felt my skin dissolving
I was disappearing, I swear
The noises faded and only a rush of
indistinct laughter remained
It was us
Our laughter lingered somewhere in space
And time could not smother it
So it kept wandering
And the things we said
They returned through my softened manners
I shared the ruins of my kingdom with you
I even tricked you into thinking
they were made of gold
"Death must be something like this" I thought
But then I assume I was being too dramatic.

## Theatrical horrors of the stars (Part II)

I have sent you that pitiable poem
It was awful
It is awful
So very dire
I wish I had told you
I finally met the man who sells gas tanks
And yells "butano"
every morning
prolonging and emphasizing
on the last "o"
as if selling the gas
depends entirely on that
last harmonious articulation
I wish I had told you
Something absolutely trivial
But all I could think of
Was having dinner with you in Litochoro
That foggy little town
Where we held each other
Where I was frightened
because you started to care
All I can think of
I have sent you that pitiable poem
I have sent you that pitiable poem
It is atrocious
Forgive me.

## Strawberries

The vacant halls
Had been asleep for years
Until we brushed our
unperishable hearts against them
Until we wandered around all night
As if we were looking for answers
As if the morning would come
And turn us into clouds of gunpowder.

Do not just stand there, charmless. Do not be a cage for oxidized memories. Do not contemplate the realm falling apart. Feel the speed. The rush of destruction. Just feel. There is nothing more to it, really.

## The Pulse of Hawberries

I'm a ghost word
I'm leftover signs of an exploded star
I'm you
I'm Agolli's canon
I'm Whitman's leaves
I'm Pizarnik's blue doll
I'm Franny and Zooey
I'm Kafka's testaments
I'm the senseless dreaming
I'm Gatsby's shirts
I'm Kadare's shattered April
I'm Holden's Jane
I'm Rogojin's knife
I'm the 'nothing without you' bit
from a movie or something
I'm Borges' bread and butter
I'm Klimt's golden allegory
I'm the non-existent space in between
I'm Emily's Nobody
I'm your grease-stained hands
I'm the ache in yearning
I'm Keats' crumpled letters
that never made it to Fanny
I'm everything
Only you shall understand
Neighbor's alarm clock goes off exactly at 7:41 a.m.
This Spanish heat is unbelievable

The sun grins at the useless fan
Pieces of conversations twirl across the room
Summertime ushers in the return of the departed
In the bleakest of circumstances
He says it is time
To be decent
To be comely.

# Saturn

Here, I hear the seagulls
At 5 am
I am eating Saturn peaches
I lie awake in bed
Feeling like a real person
Here, people are colder
And I am people
A bowl slipped from my hands
And shattered on the white floor
It cut my finger
I watched the blood
as if I had never seen blood before
And a year passed
"I love you too"
And we part
An old lady stares at us kindly
She thinks I do not struggle to know
The meaning of words
Here, there is music and cerulean waters
And you can have fun by just
walking through somber narrow alleys
And you may even see the gleam in the eyes of
people meeting again after centuries gone by
Perhaps
Hands that quiver holding a cup of coffee
Apologizing nervously
The barber shop is closed

The barber always wears plaid shirts
A different color every day
I always guess
I was right twice
He is on holiday
I wonder if he wears plaid shirts on holiday too
The old lady in the tiny bakery
Selling a lot of dry bread cubes
divided into small plastic bags
I wonder if anyone ever buys bread cubes
Here, I walked a mile in your shoes
Literally
And cursed you for taking off my boots
For giving me your shoes
For letting me drink
For leaving the keys inside the apartment
I did look crazy that day
I knew you meant well
A baby grabs my finger
The mother smiles and apologizes
The baby insists
I smile and let her hold my finger
for the next three stations
She lets go and I leave
I always leave
Here, I bought a bucket of blueberries
You called me crazy
and I told you that
I hate train rides, sometimes

That they hold too much sorrow,
as if pain is fastened to every seat

and cannot be washed off
I turn to my book
but this part of Candide is dismal
You look at me and call me crazy again
Here, I have my coffee at Two Schmucks
Because I had fourteen beers once
And could not remember Humphrey Bogart's name,
Because his fingers moved musically on my palm
Here I miss people
People who are less cold
People who are not me
People who smell of spring air.

## Around me smells like old floral deodorant and nursery rhymes

The origins of my inglorious defeat
unfolded layer by layer
A futuristic painting
with its abrupt dislocated form
You took a sample of my anguish
Examined it
How does it feel?
I want to feel like Earth
But I am trapped helium instead
I have felt the texture of your skin
I have tasted your laughter
I have inhaled your peace and
your masses of warmth
While you generously stood there
Waiting for me to emerge again
From the ice of Niflheim
From that yawning void
Into myself.

## Three Kingdoms for a Mass

Write me love letters
Paint me with the sharpest of blades
Trap me in the autumn of your consciousness
Scatter me around like light
Collect all the pieces as if you really care
Make me immortal
Tell me I am worthy of the gods
Turn me into your parish
And then
While we are sipping *chimarrão*
Tell me how
no one escapes unhappiness.

## Billycan

I saw the chink in your armor
And ran towards you wildly
Over and over
Until your armor fell apart
I dissolved in you
like noble metals do in aqua regia
You merely stood there
Always without ceremony
As if your life had been a primrose path
Every time I hurled against you
You squeezed my head closer to your chest
And ran your fingers through my hair soothingly
Assuring me I would get well
Or so I thought
You may have comforted yourself
It does make more sense
Unless you were completely self-destructive
I thought of you once
I may have seen someone
wearing something you would wear
Or having the same haircut as you
Or something absolutely human
Or it could have been nothing like it
But my brain assumed these waves
as something familiar
And I felt it for a moment
An upsurge of heat

A fervent trail of color
Oh, how startling
The disquiet
And then, it passes
I recognize the frailness of such dyes
I slouch to detach the muddled bulk of emotions
And think of how
I am still an amalgam
of all the things you were.

She did not like the way you looked at me, so attentively, the way you poured my drink and the way you arranged my necklace. She said you were "*too occupied*" with everything about me, that she would not be able to endure someone like that. She said you held my hand the whole time. I know now, she did not understand. She did not understand at all.

## Loyal sunset mutterings make me crazy

What if I leave
A frame inside your hours
What if I never slightly fitted
and parted ways
What if my surface was blown out
What if my two days to come back home
meant hiding
What if I pull myself up by my own bootstraps
and never recover
What if you are still waiting when the rain
decays the African grasslands.

## Elise

Do not think,
It is ever okay for him
To own you
Just because he shaped you
Out of ivory
Brought you to life, too
Without your consent, even
Your heart still smells like
Paris-Brest and Noisette.

## Viennese Whirls

Fireball, Spicy hara-kiri
Schnapps, Nutella, Stroh
I cannot distinguish
which is which now
All of them
Make me feel almost nothing
I become a profusion of you
Girls walk around in Christmas socks
In this almost forgotten happy hour
We drink in our biodegradable straws
In our degradable souls
And talk about meeting again some day
About how quintessential this is
About how life is just a milonga
we do not know the steps to
About how we are all worth saving.

## And that is how you defined beauty

You were right
I do not know what it is like
To end things
You said a lot of other truths too
You knew what would really hurt
And said it
I guess you did not know
How to end things either.

## Narrative of the lonely

You smothered
the only proud paper doll you had
and stood in front of the mirror
observing the warm paper cut
Nobody mentioned anything

Apparently, dogs surfing
in Huntington beach are far more amusing
The black cat had the look of a boy
who just saw his fire truck swallowed by the sea

And your boat is still sailing
on the corn flakes glass bowl
the pastel milk as still as the silence
that surrounds a sailor

Edible jewels in a box, fit for a Queen they said
Nobody cared about the old boat
I have repeated our story
so many times, it became mediocre,
so let us dance into extinction.

# Libertines

You went all *coup d'état* on my weaknesses
Overlapping voices
Profound ways
"Is he too, then, nothing more
than an ordinary human being?"
Scatter-brained
Liable to fall
That song
Reminds me for a second
I am not so wicked
Not the only one so wicked, at least
I just cannot help but think that
nobody can handle the truth
As if I were some kind of a redeemer
As if it was my right to keep it from them
In order to save them, understandably
"Am I too, then, nothing more
than an ordinary human being?"

# Fall

I had a home
I had a home
In you
Now I am wandering
My soul in my checkered socks
My heart in a raincoat
To protect it from your storm
The scent of homemade bread
Still lingered
The morning I left
You broke down crying
I did not realize
It was real
It was real
As real as Japanese honeysuckle
along the banks of the Potomac River
Distractions will not work
This time.

## Pity

October 10,
I convinced you to move on. You agreed.
October 12,
you went out with a woman that was not me
You felt guilty
I said I was happy for you
Truth is I was not happy for her
Because
She will never get to watch
The Big Friendly Giant
in that outdoors cinema with you
and rest her head on your shoulder
Inhaling the island breeze
And if she does, your mind will not be there
She will never get to sleep
under the stars with you
listening to that Moby song that made us feel
like we had constellations for dinner
She will never run to you senselessly
in that train station, unable to speak
for an hour and if she does,
it will be a different train and
you will not be wearing that green t-shirt
you were wearing the day we met
that one is still living in my closet.

## Knitting dreams and bathtubs

I ask you to live with me these days
and not think about the future, our future.
But you want us to live in a wooden house,
two dogs, three horses
you say we will go horseback riding and fishing
in our yellow raincoats and lilac rainboots
*You got it all figured out.*
*What about my poetry?*
We will have a fireplace,
speak to each other
as the warmth lights up our faces,
an attic too,
with a window facing the mountain,
You say you will build me a desk
And walnut shelves for my books
*What if my poetry doesn't fit?*
You ask me if I will let you come up and
stay with me in the attic sometimes
I say yes and I become an accomplice.
"What are you thinking about?"
"Nothing" I hardly articulate.
You seem disappointed.
"A bathtub" I add,
"I also want an old-fashioned bathtub".
Your face lights up.
"I knew you were thinking about our home.
A bathtub, of course" your eyes gleaming again.

I let myself hover with you in the mountains
for a while,
I get lost in your dream and I dream with you.
And we know the truth,
you told me that night,
when we were lying in the dark
I could only feel your heartbeat.
And we were sincere (silence and darkness
have always been a recipe for honesty),
we were real adults.
You said you know the truth,
but you are just hoping,
and asked the hopeless
if it was wrong to be hopeful.

## Lines

In what depths are you dwelling?
I cannot seem to feel the composition of you
anymore
Or your impeccable soul

In a cataclysmic painting
The world laid still
As they
Peel the flesh off our stars
and stab our sky

There by the bay, we merely watch
We have one of those talks
Half spoken half chanted
About our ephemeral valor
About the art in our encounter
About ships, giraffes and islands
And the calamity of giving up.

## You (Part I)

You will be far from Olympus
and far from home
When you learn to honor
the meek mumbling of the heart

And I will be hopscotching into the pit of
the avant-garde nothings we are having lately
Oh, how many nothings we are having lately
The skin on your arms would rise up in terror
If you knew
The amount of nothings
I have emerged myself in

Perhaps we were cosmic dust
Or just plain dust
But how unbearably lovely it was

Now a mere Mortal
With a batch of mysteries and
other significant pieces
Gracefully distant

A thought, a pause, a planet
We were
Had time perished through
the black holes of the galaxies

Had space been only gelatin
in the hands of a villain
We still are.

## Splashes

There's a rocking horse in my head
It won't rest
Its feet are tangled in a Pollock painting
There's a rocking horse in my head.

## How about tonight Josephine?

Because time is this sad sad rain
And I have no life to be what you want
I declare
I have been unscrupulous in my dreams
Because this mellow
Silence of my eyes and innocent thirst
Scorches my time of death
For this state succession
has plagued my very will to die,
Yet, I fear my heart won't survive
Let us dine with deadly nightshade wine
And fall like Macbeth's soldiers
So, how about tonight Josephine?

Of home.

# Venus

Here, I can drink tap water
and taste the forest breeze
Here, I can see the sun rising
from my bedroom window
No buildings spoiling my view
My bedsheets always smell like jasmine tea
"What did you miss?"
"Just this"
Here, I can hear my own heartbeat at night
when everything is still
Instead of the Italian couple fighting
Here, people get hurt easily
And forgive even more easily
If you apologize
Here, apologizing is rare
But actions are not
Here, it is difficult to say things and
there isn't much effort in saying
Here, things are simple
Most of the time
Here, you can still smoke inside the bars
"I missed my bed and
the glowing galaxy in the ceiling"
Here, I know every pebble
every shape the clouds make
with all their vulnerabilities
Here, watermelon is sweeter

And I can pick plums and sour cherries
right from the tree and eat them unwashed
I drink rose petal juice lying in the grass
Oh, and it is lovelier than you think
Here, there aren't many ways to love
Here, people are not born amid guitars
They are forged from hunger,
sweat and gunpowder
Here, I understand
that my mind is made for this
But my body seeks the chaotic urban disarray
And my heart
My heart is torn between the two
And it is in that fissure that I find
an agonizing happiness
Here I see people,
People who stay
People who are less and less like me
each time I come back.

## To Dritëro Agolli

I come from a village
nobody has ever heard of
My father grew up
herding his father's sheep and cattle
He exchanged his treasured radio
For a flour sack
Flour that mother turned into a home
I have soil on my eyelashes
instead of mascara
My flesh takes the appearance of corn sometimes
My top never matched my pajama bottoms
So, tell me, how can I ever save poetry
the way you did?
The acrid wind
Turns my hands into baseball gloves
To catch your chuckle
To capture life
While the floors and chairs of a bar yawn
While the steel shutters screech
Take my verses
For these verses decorate
the scratches and cuts on my skin
From collecting haricot beans
I do not know how to save poetry.

## Our old house

We wonder why it was different then,
"Something just does not feel right", you say,
and I feel it too,
"It was endless", you repeat for the tenth time,
and I clench my jaws to hold back the tears
We would count the days impatiently,
you would cut a small pine tree from the woods,
the biggest one your hands could carry,
We'd put it in a brick hole to make it stand still,
and decorated it with our spirit,
And balloons,
Nothing else
Mum would buy them for us,
and we never wondered how,
we knew she'd buy us balloons anyhow,
We would share them equally,
and tie them to the tree
and get sad when the tree blew some of them,
And oranges,
How we loved oranges,
We would peel them carefully
and put their skins on the stove,
the small room smelled like oranges and warmth,
And though the hall was dark and cold,
and "the dark room" was icy,
we had our warm room, and our pine tree,
and sweet oranges.

It was endless, the joy.
We did not question our father's absence,
we had his postcards and poems
and other kids did not get postcards,
We knew he loved us.
We did not compare our old house, its wooden stairs
and uneven floors with other polished houses,
Ours was much more than that,
it was made of stones and dirt and wood
but we would not trade it for all the concrete in the world,
Our concrete was love
Our old house was a home,
And it smelled like oranges,
like the forest,
like the cheap green fireworks
and like everything else we did not have.
It was endless, the warmth.

## Urban Blues

I am sad
So sad I cannot walk down the street
without fighting the urge to collapse
against the curb and weep like
a spoilt child on a plane isle
So sad that the homeless man without an arm
seems to be smiling at existence
or at the newspaper stand in front of him
Even his voice is joyful
as I drop the coins in his plastic food container
I want to become small
and fit into this armless man's food container
So small that even the coins falling over my head
like hail over aluminum roofs would not disturb me
I want to curl up and become air
As the day descents to dawn
my sorrow grows from within
I buy some food
but he is gone, and the newspaper stand is closed.
I stare at my mother and her worried eyes
I have to learn how to cry
without my forehead wilting
It is not easy
My mouth starts to twirl
like water rushing down a drain
I am sad
I am the homeless one

And no propolis, no crystal,
No essential oil in the world can cure that.

## Or Something Less Poetic

I haven't had any tangerines in about a year
The woman on the subway is peeling one
A pleasant balm sways
like the neck of somebody you once loved
Like a body butter you once got as a birthday present
and only used twice

I am born again
Perhaps it's the coffee I had
Or the blueberry muffin
that tasted like a polyphony
Or the dress I'm wearing
Could be any of these
Or none

I am lost, deeper than I have ever been
More than I can handle
Although it is a lie
There was nothing poetic
about the way I slammed the door and left
Today I don't want to be anything at all
Today I am just air
A tangerine fragrance
Inhale me
And I am yours.

# Noble words

Sprinkle some reality on my plate
A handful would suffice
for I have fed on dreams, too long
My mother, she warned me
"Do not fall for someone's poetry"
"If not poetry, what's worth falling for?"
I answered, not knowing

She sews me blankets made of words
Warmer than fur, colder than beer
"You taught me to rely on words"
I said to her once,
And saw pity
She did not mean to teach me that
For she loved words herself

But I did not just love words
I wanted to taste them,
smell them
and bury myself in them

And oh, how she feared
The way my mind tiptoed in the dark.

## Drown

So, we fall, injured, out of breath
And we crawl proudly
With our nails plunged in soil
The stench of rust will not fade
It has touched our very core
Corroded souls
Which cannot be polished
Endure instead,
or drown

Yes, drown
If the weight is too much
If your nails begin to bleed
If your wounds begin to open
And if you cannot hear
The shackles upon your soul
clanking, clanking, clanking

Do drown indeed
Comb your hair first
Slick it back nicely
For you must look naively dazzling
Do drown indeed

Or get up
Get up
And let life begin again

And again
Think of sweet popcorn in movie theatres
Of red wine droplets on lips
Of oat milk coffee and *pan con tomate*
Of silent loves that
have yet to announce themselves
Of Sunday mornings and tango

If you must drown
Drown in beauty
In someone's sleepy heavy eyelids
In someone's neck fragrance
Do drown in beauty
Please.

## Fluctuation

I came back
To that scent that I kind of miss
I have forgotten the feeling
Of having so many people talk at the same time

Arguing with my brother whether
Buonaparte was French or Italian or
whether his ancestors were Skanderbeg's soldiers
before escaping to Sarzana
And whether that photon of light sent back in time
might change the course of events in any way

"What's new?" I ask
"Not much" is the answer
"Same as when you left"
Yet, everything feels different

Somebody has always done something to their hair
Someone has always just recovered from the flu
And it sucks that it has not snowed yet
And the smog is getting worse
And somebody robbed a bank, but they caught him
This town is so goddamn idle
that a bank gets robbed once in a blue moon, literally

It sounds almost amusing
I cannot tell what it is

I sense the blues approaching
But I am happy everyone is well and there
It is just this humble gloominess
that has nothing to do with anything

I cannot hear my voice when I speak
and it is odd
I feel like I am muttering to myself
My face feels too warm
My mother's hand rests on my forehead

"I took out the garbage from your bedroom"
she adds as she is about to walk out the door
"What garbage?"
"That old shoebox you left by the door"
"Garbage", I repeat to myself, thinking
of all those rippled yellow notes and
plane tickets and bus tickets and
theatre tickets and concert tickets and
cans and keychains and menus and
maps and playing cards and
a first page of an old book
and a stolen ashtray
and postcards and empty envelopes and
birthday cards and
withered unknown plants
And guitar picks
And sand from a faraway island
And a lot of me
And a lot of me.

# July

Leaves of the walnut tree
bow their head
to the king of gods
they move solemnly
a song
in an unknown album
though I know who sings
I recognize the voice that asks me
to feel them in each melody
so, I do
It is the end of July
a sluggish rain
bores the soil.

## No verse is enough

I had a few verses
I had a few verses about mother
Her cashmere eyes
And the smell of burned cowmilk rice pudding
But someone opened the window
The smell is gone
And so are my verses.

## January malaise

A pillow filled with nettles
And live for truth
For me and a few others
I am in my ex's
Cleveland Cavaliers sweatpants
In my lilac room overlooking
This lilac village
And the thermal power plant
That never stops contaminating
I have been happy here
And yet, too feeble
Last night the high fever
gave me nightmares
Of you staying with me
Mother had to change my clothes
Drenched in sweat, twice
She stands by my side
With a damp white cloth
Pressing it on my forehead
I have been unkind to her at times
And yet, she never leaves
"Pluck one of my eyes out, and I will
keep looking at you with the other"
She once said to me
I get it now
I think I get it now.

## The pie

I'm on the floor
My arms are subway walls
I am making a pie
Somewhere in Barrio du Liceu
I become my mother's black dress
The one she only wore at funerals
I become the peach-colored laundry basket
I become plastic storage boxes
That I carried
In the cold
And cried
Because fairy lights do not warm
The substance the same way
Because I was sick of storage boxes
Because I was sick of temporary walls
Because I was sick of trying to make a home
Out of foldable wardrobes.

### Where I dissolve

You tiny prehistoric madman
Do not gawk at my angst
At this archaic love
That stirs and pours me
Like boiling sunlight
Over these juvenile meadows
Come hither
Seize me in my flames.

# Realization

I once ran barefoot across the field
Behind my childhood home
I stepped on a prickly chestnut shell
And cried
Those tears were uneven
Today
Tears roll like ripened apples down a hill
They are full and round and mature
I have come to realize
That matching Christmas mugs
And matching Christmas pajamas
Do not make a home.

## Bedtime stories

I cried when you read "El conejito" to me
And my eyes were dewy for months after
I was leaning on your shoulder
So stubbornly that my cheek curled up
All the way to my left eyelid
I cried from beginning to end
Your salty skin mixed with my irreversible tears
And you did not stop reading
I knew then
You would soon become my revolution
The small night lamp illuminates
Our hand holding
As we drift off to sleep.

# How I loved

I walk to school
I am ten years old
Wearing my brother's navy quilted vest
That he outgrew
The fields covered in crystal white dew
A light fog shields the once red rooftops
I cried and complained about the vest before I left
No, I wept
Just like that time my cousin cut
the eyelashes of my favorite doll
I wept
Tired of my brother's monotonous clothes
Mother was mute to my protest
I wept
There is vapor coming out of our mouths
We pretend to have
swallowed trains
Sometimes we pretend to be smoking pipes
I remove the vest
And crumple it inside my backpack
Inconsolably
It is colder without it
And a long way to arrive
But I am too proud
Too stubbornly poor
I weep no more

I know I never told you
But
That is how I loved you
With the tenacity of that ten-year old
On that unkind winter morning.

## Cyclopean masonry

I awaken bathed in Sunday letters
That two testaments could not stop
Because his thoughts were not his words
And his words were not what he wanted them to be
I awaken bathed in Talaiotic courage
And specks of light explode on my abdomen
And I do not remember who I am.

www.ingramcontent.com/pod-product-compliance
Lightning Source LLC
LaVergne TN
LVHW051130080426
835510LV00018B/2337